D0500716

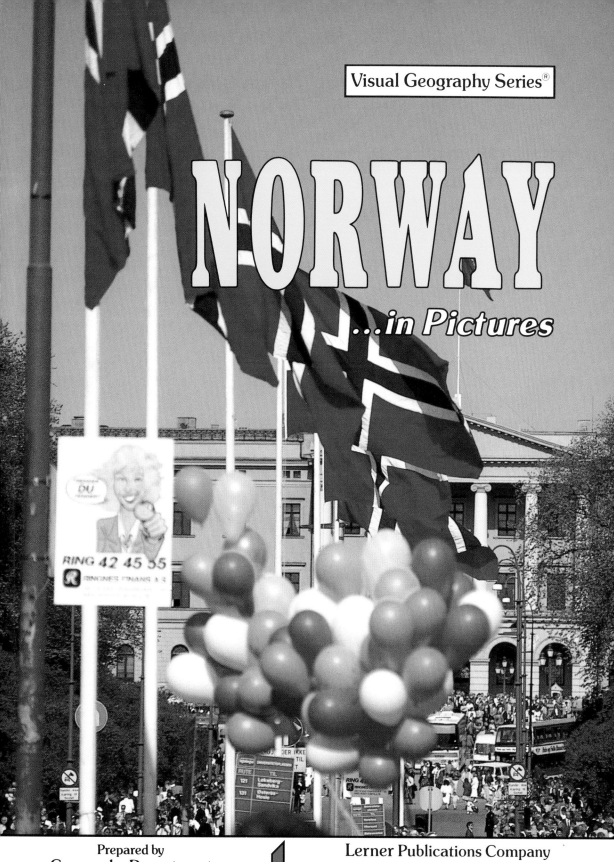

Visual Geography Series®

NORWAY

...in Pictures

Prepared by
Geography Department

Lerner Publications Company
Minneapolis

Independent Picture Service

The interior of a Norwegian church that dates from the
1100s features intricate wood carving.

This book is an all-new edition in the Visual Geography Series. Previous editions were published by
Sterling Publishing Company, New York City. The
text, set in 10/12 Century Textbook, is fully revised
and updated, and new photographs, maps, charts, and
captions have been added.

LIBRARY OF CONGRESS CATALOGING-IN-PUBLICATION DATA

Norway in pictures.

(Visual geography series)
Rev. ed. of: Norway in pictures / prepared by John B.
Burks, Jr.
Includes index.
Summary: An introduction to the geography, history,
economy, government, culture, and people of Norway.
1. Norway. [1. Norway] I. Burks, John B., 1942–
Norway in pictures. II. Lerner Publications Company.
Geography Dept. III. Title. IV. Series: Visual geog-
raphy series (Minneapolis, Minn.)
DL409.N84   1990   948.1   89-12118
ISBN 0-8225-1871-6

International Standard Book Number: 0-8225-1871-6
Library of Congress Catalog Card Number: 89-12118

VISUAL GEOGRAPHY SERIES®

Publisher
Harry Jonas Lerner
Associate Publisher
Nancy M. Campbell
Senior Editor
Mary M. Rodgers
Editors
Gretchen Bratvold
Dan Filbin
Photo Researcher
Karen A. Sirvaitis
Editorial/Photo Assistant
Marybeth Campbell
Consultants/Contributors
John G. Rice
Sandra K. Davis
Designer
Jim Simondet
Cartographer
Carol F. Barrett
Indexers
Kristine S. Schubert
Sylvia Timian
Production Manager
Gary J. Hansen

Photo by Kay Shaw Photography

At the Vigeland Sculpture Park in Oslo, two children ride
their mother horseback as they tug playfully at her braids.

Acknowledgments

Title page photo by David L. Rose

Elevation contours adapted from *The Times Atlas of
the World*, seventh comprehensive edition (New York:
Times Books, 1985).

Two special characters from the Norwegian language
have been used in this book: "å" is similar to the
English long "o," and "ø" is akin to "er."

3 4 5 6 7 8 9 10 – JR – 99 98 97 96 95

Independent Picture Service

These youngsters eagerly line up for a race at a ski school in Oslo, the nation's capital. Skiing is Norway's national sport.

Contents

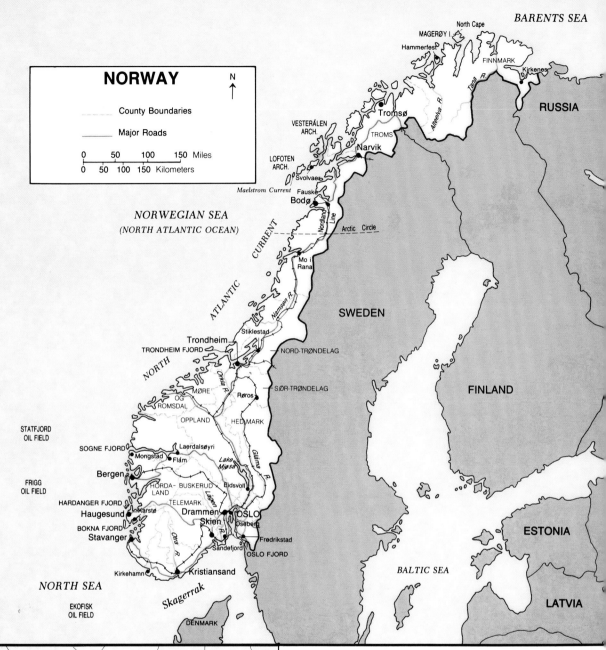

METRIC CONVERSION CHART
To Find Approximate Equivalents

WHEN YOU KNOW:	MULTIPLY BY:	TO FIND:
AREA		
acres	0.41	hectares
square miles	2.59	square kilometers
CAPACITY		
gallons	3.79	liters
LENGTH		
feet	30.48	centimeters
yards	0.91	meters
miles	1.61	kilometers
MASS (weight)		
pounds	0.45	kilograms
tons	0.91	metric tons
VOLUME		
cubic yards	0.77	cubic meters
TEMPERATURE		
degrees Fahrenheit	0.56 (*after* subtracting 32)	degrees Celsius

Tugboats tow a Norwegian oil rig out to a drilling site. The Norwegian economy depends heavily on oil deposits, which were discovered offshore in the late 1960s.

Introduction

The Kingdom of Norway—a nation located on a peninsula in northern Europe—is, along with Denmark and Sweden, part of Scandinavia. Once known as Nordweg, or the "Northern Way," the country has a rugged terrain that for centuries isolated its communities from one another. Mountains and fjords (long, narrow inlets of the sea) have made transportation and communication difficult. The sea often has provided the easiest means of travel, and most Norwegians live within a few miles of the coast.

Skilled sailors, Norwegians began to explore other areas of Europe in about A.D. 800, marking the beginning of the Viking era. As Norwegian Vikings accumulated wealth and territory abroad, they also began to unite at home. Eventually, however, the nation came under the control of its neighbors. Four centuries of Danish rule and another century of Swedish governance stifled Norway's development. When the country emerged as an independent nation in 1905, it quickly expanded its industries and focused on social welfare.

By the mid-twentieth century, Norway had many government programs to ensure equality and a high standard of living for all Norwegian citizens. The discovery of offshore oil in 1969 permitted Norway to increase social programs. Despite a sharp drop in oil revenues in the 1980s, the nation still ranks among the wealthiest in the world. Nevertheless, Norwegians are divided over trade with the rest of Europe and over environmental issues. In the coming decades, government leaders also face the challenge of building an economy that is less dependent on petroleum.

The points of a rock formation called the "Two Lovers" seem to embrace above the harbor at Svolvaer in the Lofoten Islands of northern Norway. The jagged shore behind the formation typifies the Norwegian coast. In fact, if the entire length of the coast—not counting islands—were stretched into a straight line, it would reach halfway around the world, covering more than 13,000 miles.

Independent Picture Service

1) The Land

Long and narrow, Norway covers the western and northern part of the Scandinavian Peninsula. The country has an area of 125,051 square miles, which is about the same size as the state of New Mexico. Norway also claims overseas territories. These include Svalbard—an island group in the Arctic Ocean—and Jan Mayen, a volcanic island northeast of Iceland. Bouvet Island, which is located in the South Atlantic Ocean, is also a Norwegian property. Within the Antarctic area, Norway claims Peter I Island and Queen Maud Land.

Norway spans approximately 1,086 miles in length. Because numerous fjords and peninsulas indent the jagged shore, however, Norway's coastline is much longer. The Arctic Circle divides the country almost in half. The area above this imaginary line is called the Land of the Midnight Sun because the sun shines continuously during the height of summer.

Sweden, Finland, and Russia border Norway on the east, and the North Sea, Norwegian Sea, and Barents Sea surround the rest of the country. The Skagerrak—an arm of the North Sea—extends between Norway and Denmark on the south. Norway's western coast fronts on the North Sea in the south and the North Atlantic, or the Norwegian Sea, in the north. The Barents Sea, part of the Arctic Ocean, forms the country's northern frontier. The North Cape, which is located on Norway's Magerøy Island in the Arctic Ocean, is the northernmost point in Europe.

Topography

For centuries, the Norwegian people have divided their country into four main regions. Vestlandet (West Country) and Østlandet (East Country) fill the southern third of Norway. To the north lie Trøndelag (the Trondheim region) and Nord Norge (North Norway). More recently, Sørlandet (South Country) at the southern tip of the nation has emerged as a fifth distinct region. Only about 20 percent of the country lies below an elevation of 500 feet.

VESTLANDET, ØSTLANDET, AND SØRLANDET

A north-south strip of mountains known as the Langfjellene separates Østlandet from Vestlandet in southern Norway. Several ranges make up this mountainous chain. At the northern end is the Dovrefjell, and Jotunheimen (Realm of the Giants) rises in the central mountain region. Jotunheimen contains Glittertind (8,110 feet), the highest peak in Scandinavia, and Galdhøpiggen (8,100 feet).

Photo by Hans-Olaf Pfannkuch

The town of Kirkehamn faces Norway's southern coast—a region that has warm, sunny summers.

West of Jotunheimen is Jostedalsbreen, the largest glacier in Europe outside of Iceland. To the south is the Hardangervidda, a huge elevated plateau with an average height of about 3,300 feet.

In Vestlandet, the mountains descend steeply to the sea, and many fjords cut through the region. Geologists think that the fjords were formed when glaciers deepened the rivers in the area during the Ice Age (2 million to 10,000 years ago). Sogne Fjord, Norway's longest fjord, reaches depths of 4,000 feet in some places, and its rock walls rise abruptly to more than 3,000 feet above sea level.

Lowlands lie along the southern coast of Bokna Fjord, along the lower parts of Hardanger Fjord, and on coastal islands. These areas contain most of Vestlandet's population and farmland. A *strandflat*, or rock shelf, lies just below sea level offshore. This feature forms islands, some of

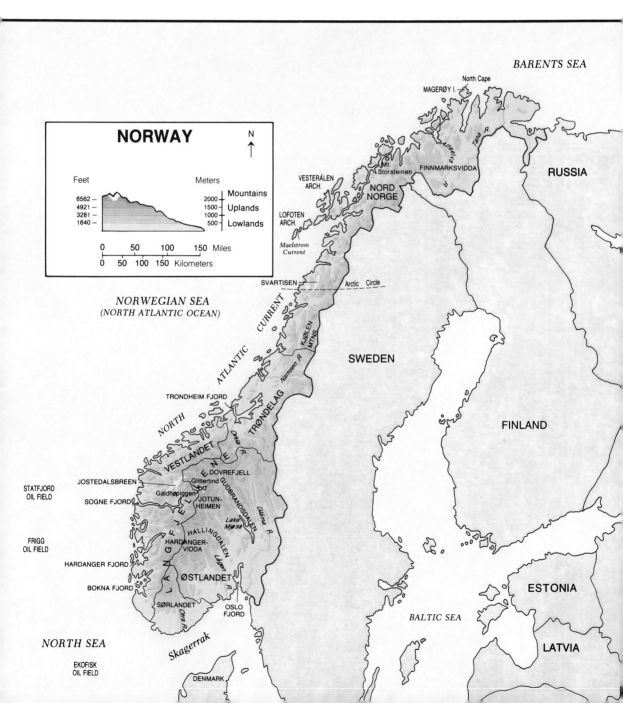

Photo by Ivan Fagre

The broad valleys of Østlandet (East Country) contain some of Norway's most fertile land. This farm is in the county of Telemark, southwest of Oslo.

which are inhabited, at points where the shelf rises just above sea level.

The gradual, eastern slopes of the Lang-fjellene make up the valleys and rolling hills of Østlandet. Some of Norway's best agricultural land lies in the lower parts of these eastern valleys, particularly around the Oslo Fjord. Several valleys, such as

Rolling hills cover much of the Trøn-delag region of central Norway.

Courtesy of Jay A. Beck

Fishing enthusiasts delight in the exciting sport offered by the Maelstrom (whirlpool) Current, which passes between two of the Lofoten Islands. The strong current carries abundant supplies of fish.

Hallingdalen and Gudbrandsdalen, connect Østlandet and Vestlandet.

Sørlandet covers the extreme southern tip of Norway and includes the city of Kristiansand. Summers in this region offer warm, sunny weather.

Svartisen—literally, "black ice"—is a glacier whose folded mass of compressed snow flows slowly into a river near Mo i Rana in northern Norway.

TRØNDELAG AND NORD NORGE

Trøndelag, located north of the highest mountains, resembles Østlandet. The broad Trondheim Fjord is the main landscape feature of this region. Many peninsulas and bays shelter the fjord from the sea, and rich farmland surrounds the waterway.

Fjords and mountains characterize the vast expanse of Nord Norge. The Kjølen Mountains extend along the border with Sweden. In northernmost Nord Norge, which faces the Arctic Ocean, the land rises up from the fjords to the Finnmarksvidda—an area of bleak mountain plateaus and glaciers.

A sparsely populated region, Nord Norge has towns primarily along the coast and on nearby islands, which are part of the strandflat. The Lofoten and Vesterålen archipelagoes, Norway's largest coastal island groups, are actually the peaks of an ancient volcanic mountain range that now lies mostly underwater. The Maelstrom Current that passes between the two outermost Lofoten islands can form dangerous whirlpools.

Rivers and Lakes

Numerous rivers in Norway have cut valleys through the mountains. Waterways that descend to the southwest from the steep western slopes are generally short, with many rapids and waterfalls. In Øst-landet, the rivers tend to be longer and travel southeastward at a gentler angle.

The longest river in Norway is the 380-mile Glåma, which begins in the Dovre-fjell and flows south into the Skagerrak at the city of Fredrikstad. Other waterways include the Alteelva and Tana in the north, the Orkla and Namsen in Trøndelag, and the Lågen and Otra in the south. For centuries, the largest rivers in southeastern Norway, such as the Glåma, have been used to float timber and to produce power for sawmills and grain mills. Although few of the waterways are navigable, they are a valuable source of hydroelectric power.

Many small lakes that were formed by glaciers dot the Norwegian countryside. The largest of these bodies of water is Lake Mjøsa, which covers 142 square miles in southeastern Norway.

Photo by A. Waldo

Dropping hundreds of feet into a fjord, this waterfall exhibits Norway's tremendous potential for hydropower.

Climate

Norway's climate is surprisingly mild for its location astride the Arctic Circle. The moderate weather is due to the North Atlantic Current, a branch of the Gulf Stream Current, which travels along the Norwegian coast. Originating in the Caribbean Sea, the waters of the Gulf Stream are warmed by the hot Caribbean sun, which makes them about 15 degrees warmer than the surrounding ocean. In winter, the Gulf Stream warms the cold westerly winds that blow toward Europe. These gusts, in turn, make coastal regions of Norway as much as 45 degrees warmer in January than the world average for the same latitude.

Hills along the fjords of Norway burst to life in the spring when the fruit trees blossom.

Independent Picture Service

As a result of this warmwater current, winter temperatures in the coastal regions usually exceed 25° F, except in the extreme north, where they may drop down to 18° F. Snow that falls along the coast melts almost immediately, and most of Norway's seaports are ice-free all year. In the summertime, however, the ocean cools the air along the western coast, and the temperature generally stays in the mid-fifties.

Inland, the differences between summer and winter become greater because the mountains shield these regions from the moderating influence of the ocean. Readings for the innermost regions range from 10° to 18° F in January. In the far north, inland temperatures fall below 10° F. Snow covers the ground for at least three months of the year in colder regions. Summers are warmest around the capital city of Oslo and along the southeastern coast, which has average temperatures in the sixties in July. The mountains and the extreme north have the coolest summer weather, with temperatures generally below 54° F.

A few areas in Norway—mainly in the upper reaches of the eastern valleys—are so dry that farmers practice irrigation. Most of the country, however, receives plenty of moisture throughout the year. Coastal regions get about 70 inches of precipitation annually, while less than 40 inches fall in areas east of the mountains. The city of Bergen on the western coast records the heaviest amounts of rainfall.

Because Norway lies so far north, the seasonal change in the number of daylight hours is much greater than it is in lands near the equator. As the earth revolves around the sun, regions close to the North and South poles alternate between facing completely into or entirely away from the sun's light. The area north of the Arctic Circle is known as the Land of the Midnight Sun because daylight lasts continuously from mid-May through July. From mid-November through January, on the other hand, the region experiences continuous darkness.

Flora and Fauna

With about 2,000 species of plants, Norway contains many forms of vegetation. A few mountain plants grow only in Norway, but most species are common to other

Even as far south as Oslo, the sun still lights the sky at 11:15 P.M. in late June.

Raspberries flourish in the Norwegian countryside.

Many Norwegians vacation at mountain cabins during the summer.

Herds of reindeer roam the snow-covered lands of northern Norway. Raised by the Lapps—an ethnic group of northern Norway, Sweden, and Finland—the animals have suffered the effects of environmental pollution in recent years, and their numbers have dwindled.

countries as well. The richest vegetation in Norway is found in the southeast along Oslo Fjord and near large lakes such as Mjøsa. Mushrooms and wild berries—including blueberries, lingonberries, and cranberries—grow in wooded areas. Rare outside Scandinavia is the cloudberry (a relative of the blackberry), which hikers gather in mountain areas.

Norwegian forests, which cover more than one-fifth of the land area, abound in fir and pine. Deciduous (leaf-shedding) forests consisting of oak, ash, hazel, elm, and linden are located in the south and southwest. In some places, birch, yew, and evergreen holly thrive. The coasts and the eastern and central valleys are thick with Scotch pine and Norway spruce. Birch, alder, aspen, and mountain ash also grow in these regions.

In the far north and at high elevations are tundra regions—barren lands that support only hardy dwarf shrubs and wildflowers. Animal life in these areas includes reindeer, polar foxes, polar hare, wolves, wolverines, and lemmings. Elk, deer, foxes, otters, and marten inhabit the south and southeast.

About 300 species of birds nest in Norway for at least part of the year. Some of these—certain kinds of hawks, falcons, and eagles, for example—are endangered species. The law protects white-tailed and golden eagles. Millions of sea birds—including puffins, gulls, gannets, and fulmars—breed on cliffs that overlook the ocean.

Both freshwater and saltwater fish abound in Norway. Salmon, trout, grayling, perch, and pike swim in the rivers and lakes. Herring, cod, and mackerel are among the species that inhabit the coastal waters.

Cities and Towns

Although Oslo is Norway's only major urban center, several smaller cities dot the countryside. Stavanger, Kristiansand, Drammen, Skien, Tromsø, and Bodø have populations between 30,000 and 100,000. Hammerfest (population 7,500) is the northernmost town in the world.

OSLO

The capital city of Oslo sits at the inner tip of Oslo Fjord, which stretches 60 miles northward from the southern coast. King Harald III founded Oslo in about A.D. 1050. After a fire destroyed the city in 1624, King Christian IV rebuilt it and residents renamed it Christiania in honor of their ruler. The original name, Oslo, was restored in 1925.

Oslo has served as Norway's capital since the nation achieved complete independence from Sweden in 1905. It is also the country's principal commercial, industrial, and cultural center. With a popu-

lation of about 473,000, the city covers 175 square miles. Forests and lakes take up more than two-thirds of this area, which makes Oslo an ideal recreation center. Major industries in the capital include shipbuilding and the production of chemicals, machinery, metal, and paper.

Karl Johansgate, the main street that runs through the middle of the city, passes the stately Grand Hotel, the yellow-brick Parliament Building, the University of Oslo, and the National Theater. The thoroughfare stretches from the Central Railway Station to the gardens of the Royal Palace. Several museums and galleries—the National Gallery, the Vigeland Sculpture Park, the open-air Folk Museum, and the Viking Ships Museum, for example—attract both Norwegians and foreigners.

SECONDARY CITIES

Set in a valley at the foot of seven mountains, Bergen is Norway's second largest city, with a population of about 218,000. Founded in 1070 by King Olav III, Bergen has many historic buildings that date back to the twelfth century. The city remains rich in tradition, despite several fires throughout its history and severe damage during World War II (1939–1945). The chief seaport of western Norway, Bergen is a cultural, fishing, industrial, and shipping center. Factories in the city manufacture steel, ships, fishing equipment, processed food, forest products, and electrical machinery.

The oldest city in Norway, Trondheim has more than 140,000 residents, which makes it the third largest urban area in the country. Founded in 997 by King Olav I, Trondheim (then known as Nidaros) served as Norway's capital until 1380. The city's most important landmark is Nidarosdomen, an eleventh-century cathedral built over the tomb of King Olav II, Norway's patron saint. A commercial hub for the surrounding agricultural area, Trondheim is also an export center for copper, iron ore, timber, and fish.

Independent Picture Service

Thousands of puffins, or sea parrots, nest on the rocks in the Lofoten Islands each summer. The birds are expert swimmers and divers.

People stroll down Karl Johansgate, the main street in the capital city of Oslo.

Colorful buildings featuring traditional architectural styles flank the streets of Bergen, an important Norwegian trading center since the thirteenth century.

16

The early Norwegians carved fierce-looking animal heads on the tops of posts to protect themselves from evil spirits. Archaeologists uncovered this post, which dates from about A.D. 850, at Oseberg. It was found in a burial ship that contained a Viking queen, along with objects for her to use in her afterlife.

2) History and Government

Although the first written records of Norwegian history date from about A.D. 800, archaeologists have traced evidence of human activity in the country back to 8000 or 9000 B.C. By that time, most of the ice from the last glacial period had receded from Norway.

The oldest finds come from Finnmark, the northernmost county in Norway, and from Møre in northwestern Vestlandet. The inhabitants of these areas probably hunted and fished for food, and they fashioned tools from bone, antlers, and stone. Although their origins are unknown, these

A rock carving that dates from the Bronze Age, which began around 2000 B.C., depicts early Norse ships.

peoples may have reached Norway from across the narrow Kola Peninsula in northern Russia. Another route might have brought the newcomers from central Europe by way of Denmark and Sweden, which at that time were connected to each other by land.

The Rise of Permanent Settlements

Until about 3000 B.C., the peoples of Norway lived in tents or in mountain caves along the coast. They kept only one kind of domestic animal—dogs—and lived by hunting and fishing. Between 3000 and 1500 B.C., warlike Germanic groups migrated to Norway. From them the local inhabitants learned to attach handles to their axes, which made the tools more efficient in work and in battle. During this period, the people also began to keep cattle and to grow grain. As farming became a way of life, the inhabitants of Norway no longer needed to roam in search of food.

Permanent farming settlements arose along the coast and around lakes. Fjords and mountains isolated these communities from one another. As a result, they became independent realms, each with its own leader. Eventually, aristocracies (small, ruling classes) developed, and kings emerged from these privileged groups to head the communities. By the 700s A.D., about 30 small kingdoms existed in Norway.

The Viking Age

After A.D. 600, Norway entered a period of rapid population growth, perhaps because Germanic peoples had moved to Scandinavia in the previous two centuries. The population increase led to shortages of farmland, and the inhabitants began to take an interest in other regions. By about

The front end of the Viking burial ship found at Oseberg is intricately carved.

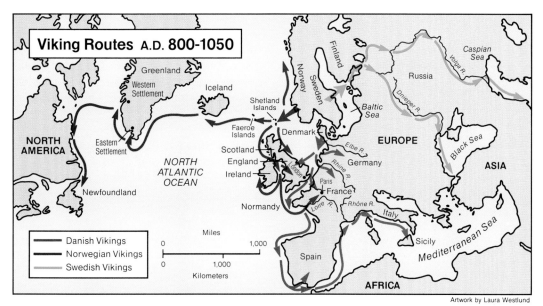

Viking Routes A.D. 800-1050

Danish Vikings
Norwegian Vikings
Swedish Vikings

Miles
0   1,000
0   1,000
Kilometers

Artwork by Laura Westlund

Between about A.D. 800 and 1050, the Vikings sailed in three main directions from Scandinavia (Norway, Denmark, and Sweden). The Danes went south, raiding Germany, France, England, Spain, and the Mediterranean coast. Initially the Norwegians followed the same course, but they soon focused their attention westward, on Iceland, Greenland, and North America. The Swedes traveled to eastern Europe.

800 (and possibly much sooner), Norwegians, Danes, and Swedes began to travel abroad, conquering territory and expanding their markets. The Scandinavians of this period, which lasted until about 1050, later became known as Vikings. The term may have come from *vik,* the Norse word for "fjord" or "bay." It could also be a form of the Old English word *wic,* which means a soldier or trader.

Warlike raids, which small groups carried out against various other European communities, marked the first hundred years of the Viking Age. These acts gave the Vikings a reputation of being pirates. Gradually, however, their expeditions abroad became larger and more organized, with armies and navies under the command of chieftains.

Despite their aggressive reputation, not all Vikings were warriors. The majority worked most of the time as farmers or in occupations such as shipbuilding, metal working, or fishing. Viking traders sailed to many parts of the world in swift,

lightweight wooden vessels that ranked among the best boats of their time. In fact, trade eventually became the primary activity of the Vikings.

VIKING EXPEDITIONS

One of the first recorded Viking attacks occurred in 793, when Norwegians plundered a monastery on the island of Lindisfarne, off the eastern coast of England. After that, Norwegians began raiding England, Ireland, the Isle of Man, and Scotland. Ireland, with its fertile land and rich churches, was a choice target for attack. During the mid-800s, Norwegian raiders also looted and burned towns in France, Italy, and Spain.

By the late 800s, Viking expeditions had become more peaceful. The paths opened up by earlier pirate activities became trade routes. Some Norwegians turned to the North Atlantic, exploring and immigrating to uninhabited islands—the Faeroes and Iceland. From Iceland, a Norwegian explorer named Eric Thorvaldson (Eric the

Red) sailed to Greenland in 982, and a few years later he established two settlements there. Eventually, Norway added the Faeroes, Iceland, and Greenland to its kingdom.

In about 1000, Leif Ericsson, son of Eric the Red, led an expedition farther west and landed on the eastern coast of North America. Ericsson called the territory Vinland and established a settlement in what is now the Canadian province of Newfoundland. This first European colony on the American continent, however, was soon abandoned because of attacks from local inhabitants. Nevertheless, Greenlanders continued expeditions to Vinland to gather timber until the mid-fourteenth century. After the fifteenth century, the Norwegian population on Greenland died out, and Norway lost contact with the North American region.

ATTEMPTS TO UNIFY NORWAY

Shortly before 900, King Harald Fairhair (Harald I), from a realm in southeastern

Norway, defeated many regional chieftains and kings. The unity he achieved, however, was short-lived. After his death in 933, his sons divided the kingdom, with Eric Bloodaxe as the supreme ruler. Conflict erupted among the heirs, and many of the regional leaders refused to surrender their independence. While these domestic struggles were occurring, both Denmark and Sweden sought Norwegian territory.

Olav Tryggvason (Olav I), a great-grandson of Harald I, ascended the throne in 995. As a youth, Olav I had lived in England, where he adopted the Roman Catholic religion. Once he became king, Olav I tried to impose his Christian faith on his subjects, killing those who would not accept it. In 1000, at the naval battle of Svold, the forces of Denmark and Sweden united with dissatisfied Norwegian leaders to defeat and kill Olav I. The victors divided the land among themselves.

In 1015 Olav Haraldsson (Olav II) drove out the foreigners, reunited Norway, and made himself king. Olav II continued to

Eric the Red led a crew of Norwegians west from Iceland late in the tenth century. They discovered the barren shores of Greenland and established a colony there.

A popular subject of church murals throughout Scandinavia, King Olav II is the patron saint of Norway. During his reign from 1015 to 1030, Olav II brutally forced Norwegians to convert to Christianity. He faced a violent end—symbolized by the man with the ax—at the Battle of Stiklestad in 1030. He has since been honored for bringing the Christian faith to his country.

force Christianity upon Norwegians. As he increased his power, Olav II created many enemies among the nobles. This group united with Canute II, king of Denmark and England, and in 1030 killed Olav II at the Battle of Stiklestad, northeast of Trondheim. Olav's death put Norway in Danish hands.

Danish rulers imposed heavy taxes, and Norwegians grew discontented with foreign control. They began to think of Olav II as a hero for his efforts to unite the country, despite his cruel enforcement of Christianity. Much later, Catholic authorities in Rome elevated Olav II to sainthood. By proclaiming him a saint, the church aroused even greater national pride among Norwegians, and Christianity became firmly rooted in the country.

Three Centuries of Self-rule

After King Canute died in 1035, Norwegians hailed Olav II's son Magnus as Norway's king. Magnus I united Norway and Denmark under his rule. For the next three centuries, Norwegian kings ruled Norway. During this period, the Roman Catholic Church grew in power, foreign trade expanded, and Norwegian religious and trading centers grew to be important cities. Political chaos and bitter struggles for

Nidaros Cathedral was built between 1150 and 1300 on the banks of the Nid River in Trondheim. Scandinavia's largest medieval building, the structure rises above the grave of Saint Olav. For centuries, Christian pilgrims from all over Europe have visited the site.

Courtesy of Kristine Berglund

royal power also developed, since all the sons of a king had equal rights to succession.

From 1130 to 1240, civil wars ravaged the country as nobles from different regions unsuccessfully tried to gain the throne. In 1184 Sverre Sigurdsson became king and reestablished the role of the monarch as the supreme ruler of the land—a move that weakened the power of the church. As a result, religious leaders opposed Sverre's reign, and another round of civil wars began. Haakon Haakonsson (Haakon IV), Sverre's successor, restored

lasting peace in 1240, when he killed his main rival at a battle near Trondheim.

In 1250 Haakon IV granted trading privileges to a group of northern German merchant cities known as the Hanseatic League. Gradually, this organization took control of Norwegian trade, and the country depended on the league for imports of grain. The monarchs of this period increased their power and restricted succession to the throne to the oldest legitimate son of a king.

When Haakon Magnusson (Haakon V) became king in 1299, he established his

A fourteenth-century woodcut depicts a visit to a patient suffering from the plague. Sometimes called the Black Death because black spots of blood formed under the skin, the plague that swept through Europe in the 1300s killed one-fourth of the continent's population.

royal residence in Oslo. Haakon V built several castles to help fortify the country since the old naval defense system had fallen apart. To ensure his own power, Haakon V eliminated the titles of earl and baron from the aristocracy and ruled without the advice of nobles. As a result, the nobility gradually declined.

Haakon V had no male heirs. When he died in 1319, the throne went to the son of his daughter, who had married a Swedish prince. Magnus Eriksson (Magnus VII) thus became king of both Norway and Sweden. Magnus VII lived in Sweden, however, and neglected Norwegian affairs. In 1349 and 1350, the bubonic plague swept across Norway, killing at least half

Photo by Philadelphia Museum of Art, SmithKline Beckman Corporation Fund

Photo by Ivan Fagre

Buildings used as warehouses by the Hanseatic League line the waterfront in Bergen. A confederation of northern German cities, the league controlled much of European trade during the 1300s and 1400s. Towns that refused to join the league were unable to sell their goods in profitable markets.

the population. Survivors of the epidemic faced famine and severe economic problems. To satisfy Norwegian demands for more consideration of their needs, Magnus VII gave the Norwegian throne to his son Haakon in 1355. Haakon VI was the last king of an independent Norway until 1905.

Union with Denmark

After Haakon VI died in 1380, his wife, Margrete, who was the ruler of Denmark, became the queen of Norway as well. In 1388, amid political instability in Sweden, Swedish nobles elected her to rule their country. In 1397 Margrete formally united Norway, Denmark, and Sweden in the Union of Kalmar. Sweden revolted against Danish rule several times and eventually broke away from the union in 1523. Norway, however, remained under Danish control for the next four centuries.

During the union with Denmark, Norway grew weaker politically as Denmark increased its strength. In 1536 Denmark declared Norway a Danish province and dissolved the Norwegian national council, thereby stripping the country of its voice in Norwegian affairs. Denmark also made Lutheranism—a newly formed sect that had broken away from the Roman Catholic Church—the official religion of Norway.

Despite Danish control, Norway's economy began to prosper in the sixteenth century as Norwegians discovered a European market for their vast reserves of

Akershus Castle in Oslo is one of several fortresses built during the reign of Haakon V (1299-1319). The king sought to strengthen the country's weak defense system.

These eighteenth-century farm buildings *(left and below),* are rough-hewn and sparsely furnished. Elaborate wood carving and a style of painting called *rosmaling* (rose painting) add warmth to the simple structures.

Independent Picture Service

Independent Picture Service

timber. As a result, the Norwegian shipping industry expanded rapidly during the sixteenth and seventeenth centuries. A class of wealthy townspeople arose, and the number of port cities increased.

Norway prospered in peace throughout the eighteenth century, until the territorial goals of the French general Napoleon Bonaparte pitted nations against one another. When Napoleon set out to conquer Europe during the Napoleonic Wars (1804–1814), Denmark sided with France against Great Britain. Britain, which had been Norway's chief trading partner, used its naval forces to prevent ships from landing in Norway. Norwegian trade stopped, and many Norwegians starved. Because the blockade cut off Norway from Denmark, Norwegians began to manage their own affairs, and they secretly resumed trade with the British.

Sweden, an ally of Britain, defeated Denmark in 1813. According to the Treaty of Kiel, Denmark gave Norway to Sweden but kept Norway's island colonies—Iceland, Greenland, and the Faeroes. At first Norway refused to recognize the treaty. Instead it declared independence and adopted a Norwegian constitution on May 17, 1814. Sweden, however, would not accept Norwegian independence and attacked and quickly defeated Norwegian troops. In November 1814, the Norwegian Storting (parliament) accepted King

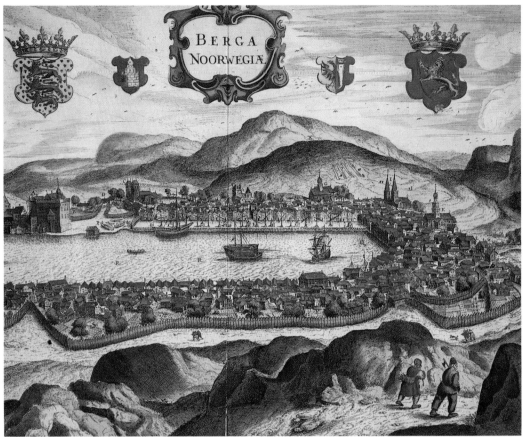

Bergen thrived as Norway's chief commercial port during the centuries of foreign control. Sailing ships—such as those in this sixteenth-century illustration—carried goods to ports throughout the world. In the second half of the nineteenth century, the volume of exports transported by the country's merchant marine more than quadrupled, and steamships began to replace sailing vessels.

Charles XIII of Sweden as Norway's ruler. Charles promised to uphold the Norwegian constitution.

Union with Sweden

Although Sweden controlled Norway's foreign affairs, the colonial power granted Norway a great deal of internal independence. A Norwegian cabinet advised the Swedish king on matters that affected Norway, and the Norwegian Storting established self-government and improved the nation's economy.

During the nineteenth century, Norway began to develop textile, paper, and fish-canning industries. At the same time, the nation constructed railways and roads, which made it easier to transport these products throughout the country. Expansion of the merchant marine, which shipped goods around the globe, made Norway active in world trade. By 1870 Norway's merchant marine had become the third largest in the world. These economic developments transformed Norwegian agriculture into a business in which farmers produced crops for sale rather than just to feed their families.

Despite these improvements, economic growth could not keep pace with a population that more than doubled during the nineteenth century. The 1880s were especially hard years, and many people could not find jobs. Between 1866 and 1915, over 600,000 Norwegians immigrated to North America in search of jobs and cheap, fertile land. No other country except Ireland lost as high a percentage of its population to U.S. immigration.

The rapid departure of so many Norwegians forced the government to examine its policies. The Storting enacted social legislation in the late nineteenth and early twentieth centuries partly to satisfy Norwegians who were tempted to emigrate. Democratic reforms improved the

Faced with severe economic hardship, thousands of Norwegians immigrated to the New World in the late 1800s. This couple settled in the state of Minnesota.

Courtesy of G. Bratvold

Courtesy of D. Bratvold

Entire Norwegian families commonly left for the United States in the late nineteenth century. Many farms—such as this one that was abandoned by emigrants—eventually fell into ruin.

Johan Sverdrup was instrumental in weakening the union between Sweden and Norway. After serving in parliament for many years, he became prime minister of Norway in 1884.

Henrik Ibsen, the father of modern drama, wrote plays during the late 1800s that presented social problems in a realistic way. Among his best-known works are *A Doll's House*, *An Enemy of the People*, and *Hedda Gabler*.

legal status of poor people, extended the rights of women, and gave the working class greater power.

In 1884 the liberal Venstre (Left) and conservative Høyre (Right) political parties were formed. A few years later, the Norwegian Labor party entered the political arena. Johan Sverdrup, founder of the Venstre party and president of the Storting, united Norwegian peasants and encouraged them to speak up for their needs. The right to vote was extended to all men over the age of 25 in 1898, and women gained equal voting rights in 1913.

Along with the nineteenth-century liberal democratic movement arose nationalistic sentiments. Norwegians grew increasingly discontented with their inferior political position in the union with Sweden. They sought greater freedom, particularly in foreign affairs. Literature and intellectual activity began to reflect a distinct Norwegian identity. Bjørnstjerne Bjørnson, who wrote the Norwegian national anthem, Henrik Wergeland, and Henrik Ibsen were among the spokespeople for this cultural rebirth.

Struggle for Independence

As Norwegians strengthened their national identity and political power, they grew bolder in their demands on Sweden. In 1892 the Venstre majority in the Storting passed a resolution to establish an independent consular service. This meant Norway could send its own representatives to foreign countries to protect Norwegian business interests. The Swedish king Oscar II vetoed the resolution, and negotiations about the terms of the Swedish-Norwegian union led nowhere. In response, Norwegian leaders decided to strengthen their position by building up their military.

King Oscar II still refused to grant consular service to Norway, and in 1905 the Norwegian cabinet resigned. Because the Norwegian constitution allowed the king to exercise royal power only through a cabinet, the resignation of the cabinet left King Oscar II powerless in Norway. In effect, Norway no longer had a king, and the union between Sweden and Norway therefore no longer existed.

At first the Swedish government refused to dissolve the union, but it agreed to reconsider the matter if a general election in Norway proved that a majority of the Norwegian people desired independence. Norwegians voted almost unanimously for self-rule, and Sweden agreed to recognize Norwegian independence in September 1905.

After debating whether to establish a monarchy or a republic, a majority of Norwegians voted to install a king. Since the Norwegians had no royalty of their own, they elected Prince Carl of Denmark as their king. He took the name Haakon VII, thereby continuing a line of kings that had ended with the formation of the union with Denmark upon the death of Haakon VI in 1380.

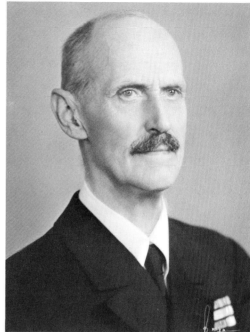

In 1905 Norwegians welcomed Prince Carl, who left Denmark to become King Haakon VII of Norway. Haakon VII guided the nation until his death in 1957.

At Eidsvoll Manor, Norwegians signed their constitution on May 17, 1814. The document provided the basis for the nation's independence, which was gained in 1905.

In the decade before Norway gained complete self-rule, Norwegian leaders built up the country's military power in the hopes of frightening Sweden into giving up control. This cannon watches over Oslo from Akershus Castle.

The Early 1900s

During the early years of independence, Norway underwent a rapid transition from an economy founded on agriculture to one based on manufacturing and trade. Industries that processed metals and chemicals developed in addition to the existing textile and food-processing plants. Hydroelectric power stations were built along the nation's many rivers to fuel the emerging factories.

The newly independent nation also made great strides in social legislation, education, and political liberties, setting an example that many European countries would follow later. Norway became famous for welfare policies such as unemployment benefits, retirement pensions, and liberal laws concerning divorce and illegitimacy (children born out of wedlock).

During World War I (1914–1918), Norway, Sweden, and Denmark agreed to remain neutral and to cooperate for their mutual interest. The friendship established during this period continued after the war.

When the war ended, Norway experienced an economic decline, and a worldwide depression in 1929 worsened the nation's financial situation. One-fourth to one-third of the nation's workers were unemployed during the 1930s.

World War II

When World War II began in 1939, Norway maintained its traditional policy of neutrality. The Germans forced Norway into the war, however, when they invaded the country on April 9, 1940. Assisted by Vidkun Quisling and other disloyal Norwegian army officers, the Germans attacked all Norway's important ports. After two months of fighting, Norway surrendered, and King Haakon VII and his cabinet fled

In the early twentieth century, Norwegians began to hunt whales in Antarctic waters. The development of huge factory ships meant that whalers no longer needed to depend on land bases near their hunting grounds to process their catch. A revolving monument in Sandefjord—a Norwegian community that prospered with the rise of Antarctic whaling—captures the excitement of harpooning a whale. In the 1960s, Norway began to reduce its whaling activities to preserve the species. In the 1980s, the country halted commercial whale hunting.

Independent Picture Service

Courtesy of Harlan V. Anderson

Photo by Hans-Olaf Pfannkuch

The development of railroads *(left)* and hydropower *(right)* in the early twentieth century enabled Norway to build new industries.

to London, where they formed a government-in-exile. Germany installed Josef Terboven as its commissioner in Norway. The Norwegian people strongly resisted the repressive measures of the German occupation. They also aided the efforts of the Allied powers against Germany.

On May 8, 1945, after Germany was defeated elsewhere, the German forces in Norway surrendered. King Haakon returned to Norway on June 7, the fortieth anniversary of Norwegian independence. In order to punish traitors, the government restored the death penalty, which had been abolished in 1876. Quisling, whose name had become an international word for traitor, was tried in court and executed for treason along with about 25 other Norwegians. About 10,000 Norwegians had died during the war, about half the merchant fleet had sunk, and the northern counties of Troms and Finnmark lay largely in ruins.

Norwegian officials show Vidkun Quisling *(center)* a mass grave containing the bodies of Norwegians murdered by Nazis and followers of Quisling during World War II (1939-1945). After the war, Quisling was executed for treason.

German attacks destroyed many parts of Narvik and other towns in northern Norway during World War II.

Members of the Norwegian *Storting*, or parliament, are elected every four years. In the nineteenth and twentieth centuries, this political body has enacted many social laws that have improved Norway's standard of living.

Norway's foreign minister during World War II, Trygve Lie also served as the United Nations' secretary-general from 1946 to 1953.

Postwar Developments

After the war, Norway became a charter member of the United Nations (UN) in 1945, and the Norwegian Trygve Lie became the UN's first secretary-general. In 1949 Norway also joined the North Atlantic Treaty Organization (NATO), a regional defense alliance.

Aided by loans from the United States, Norway rebuilt its industries and its merchant fleet. The government, led by the Labor party, carefully planned the entire economy. The nation strengthened its position in international markets and redistributed wealth more equally among its citizens. By the 1950s, the Norwegian economy was thriving as it shifted from an emphasis on industries to a focus on services such as health care and banking.

In the mid-1950s, the Nordic countries (Denmark, Finland, Iceland, Norway, and Sweden) formed the Nordic Council. This

33

King Olav V *(left)* and his son, Crown Prince Harald *(right)* celebrate Constitution Day on May 17, 1978. Upon Olav's death in January 1991, Harald succeeded to the throne, becoming the first Norwegian-born king since the fourteenth century.

With the discovery of oil in Norwegian waters in 1969, the nation began building drilling equipment, tankers, and refineries.

organization has fostered much cooperation between the member countries, primarily on economic, social, and cultural issues. To further secure its well-being, Norway and six other countries formed an economic union called the European Free Trade Association (EFTA) in 1959.

New social legislation accompanied economic growth and greatly improved the welfare of Norwegians. In 1966 the Storting passed the National Insurance Act—one of the most important reforms in Norwegian history. A social security plan, this program covers retirement pensions and job retraining. The act also gives aid to mothers, orphans, widows, widowers, and handicapped persons.

During the 1970s, the state began to produce petroleum and natural gas, which an exploration team had discovered in the Norwegian section of the North Sea. Since then, the economy has depended on the export of oil and natural gas. While fossil fuel production is predicted to rise, the reliance on these products for the nation's income threatens economic stability because the supply is limited and because oil prices are often unpredictable.

Recent Events

Throughout the 1980s, the Norwegian government adopted strict antipollution laws, and Prime Minister Gro Harlem Brundtland became an international leader of the debate on environmental issues. Yet severe pollution continues to affect Norwegian lakes, forests, and wildlife. Pollution from foreign sources, such as factory smoke from Great Britain, has caused strained relations between Norway and its neighbors. In addition, Norwegian leaders disagree on the economic costs and benefits of stricter environmental laws.

Norwegians are also sharply divided over joining the European Union (EU), an economic partnership of European countries. Brundtland, who has ruled the country for three terms (except for a short out-of-office stint from 1989 to 1990), favors joining the EU. Many Norwegians, however, are concerned about losing control over their natural resources, especially profitable fishing waters and oil reserves. Norway negotiated an agreement in 1994 that would secure Norway's rules about management and conservation if they were to join the EU. Many believe that it would be economically unsound to remain outside of the EU. Other Scandinavian countries have decided to join, but no one knows for certain what Norway will choose to do.

The Norwegian Storting meets in this building, which was built in Oslo in the 1860s.

Government

Norway is a constitutional and hereditary monarchy, and only males are allowed to inherit the throne. Although the Constitution of 1814 has been changed many times, its basic features remain the same. The king's role is mainly ceremonial, but he has influence as a symbol of national unity. The monarch is the supreme commander of the Norwegian armed forces. He also is the head of the Church of Norway, to which he and at least half of the executive cabinet must belong.

A government official called an ombudsman investigates complaints made by

Photo by UPI/Bettmann Newsphotos

Gro Harlem Brundtland, Norway's first female prime minister, took office for the third time in 1990. She has been active in global environmental issues.

Photo by Liv Dahl

Adopted by the Storting in 1821, the Norwegian flag is much used on holidays—especially on May 17—and on family occasions.

citizens about governmental actions or decisions. The office was established to provide an impartial and informal method of handling unfair treatment against individuals.

Executive power is exercised through a prime minister and a cabinet. The king appoints the prime minister, who is usually the leader of the political party holding the most seats in the Storting. The prime minister, in turn, appoints 17 cabinet ministers, who head the various governmental departments. Cabinet members sit in the Storting, but they do not vote.

All Norwegian citizens who are 18 or older can participate in parliamentary elections, which are held every four years. Each of Norway's 19 counties elects 4 to 15 Storting members, depending on the size of the local population. The Storting consists of one house, but its 157 members form two sections—the Lagting and the Odelsting—to discuss and vote on proposed legislation. If the two sections do not agree on a piece of legislation, it can be approved by a two-thirds majority of the entire parliament. Some matters can be decided only by the entire Storting.

The highest judicial body in Norway is the supreme court, which consists of a president and 17 judges. Below this, five regional courts of appeal hear the most serious cases as well as appeals of decisions made by county and town courts. Conciliation councils handle civil suits, and county and town courts determine criminal cases. The king appoints judges to all of the courts except the conciliation courts, whose members are elected locally.

For administrative purposes, Norway is divided into 19 *fylker,* or counties—one of which is the city of Oslo. Each fylke except Oslo has a governor appointed by the king. The fylker, in turn, are divided into rural and urban *kommuner,* or districts. Community councils, which are elected every fourth year, run the local districts. County councils consist of members of the community councils.

On *Syttende Mai,* or May 17th, Norwegians throughout the country dress in their national costumes and walk in parades.

3) The People

Most of Norway's 4.3 million inhabitants are closely related to the Danes and the Swedes. These three Scandinavian peoples are descended from ancient groups that migrated to the region. Their ancestors came from lands east of the Baltic Sea, from around the Mediterranean Sea, or from the European Alps. Throughout the centuries, Norwegians intermarried with other groups, taking on various physical traits from these different peoples. Contrary to the popular image of fair-haired Norwegians, many of the nation's people have dark hair and brown eyes.

In Nord Norge reside the Lapps, an ethnic minority numbering about 20,000. The Lapps are thought to be the first inhabitants of Norway. They arrived from central Asia thousands of years ago and have darker skin and a shorter stature than most Norwegians. Their language is related to Finnish.

Traditionally, the Lapps are a nomadic people who follow herds of reindeer in the northern regions of Norway, Sweden, Finland, and Russia. Many modern Lapps, however, have settled in fishing or farming villages, and they now more commonly marry outside their ethnic community. Environmental issues—such as acid rain and rechanneling water to create hydropower—are threatening the existence of the reindeer, and therefore the lifestyle of the Lapps.

Wearing traditional clothing, two Lapp boys hold hands at recess.

Although in many ways Lappish lifestyles have remained unchanged for centuries, Lapps now enjoy the modern convenience of grocery shopping at the local store.

This Pakistani man is one of thousands of south Asian immigrants who have settled in Norway to take advantage of the social and economic opportunities offered by the government's welfare programs. Some Norwegians have begun to question whether the government can afford to extend benefits to foreigners living in the country.

Immigrants from southern Europe and various Third World countries make up another minority in Norway. The nation depends on these foreigners to help fill its work force. Between 1978 and 1987, the number of new arrivals in the country nearly doubled. Many foreign workers and their families have taken up permanent residence in Norway, where they can enjoy a greatly improved standard of living. Even with these newcomers, the country has a population density of only 33 persons per square mile. About 70 percent of the nation's people live in cities.

Social Welfare

The government of Norway provides its citizens with many welfare services. Indeed, the nation has been a world leader in the establishment of state-funded health care, housing, employment benefits, retirement plans, and other services. Based on ideals of equality and justice, Norwegian legislation guarantees the right to employment, to a place to live, to education, to

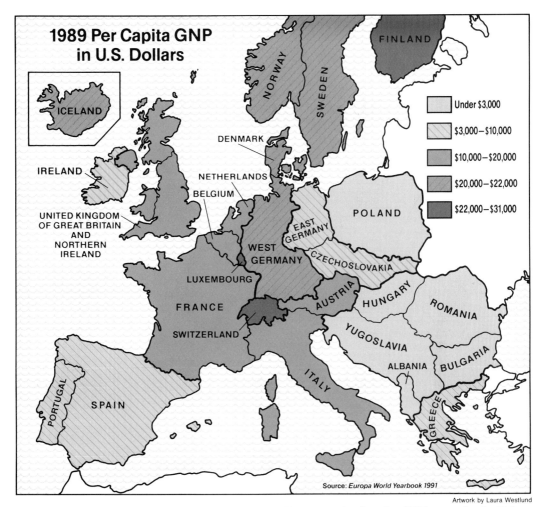

1989 Per Capita GNP in U.S. Dollars

Under $3,000	
$3,000–$10,000	
$10,000–$20,000	
$20,000–$22,000	
$22,000–$31,000	

Source: *Europa World Yearbook 1991*

Artwork by Laura Westlund

This map compares the average wealth per person—calculated by gross national product (GNP) per capita—for 26 European countries. The GNP is the value of all goods and services produced by a country in a year. To arrive at the GNP per capita, each nation's total GNP is divided by its population. In 1989 Norway's GNP was more than $21,000. By the mid-1990s it was over $26,000—among the highest figures in the world—which, combined with government welfare programs, has enabled the nation's people to lead comfortable, healthy lives.

social security, and to health and hospital services. Discrimination because of race, religion, gender, or political beliefs is prohibited. The government funds the welfare system through taxes and insurance, taking from those who earn the most and giving to those who need assistance. The result is a socialist society in which few people are very rich or very poor.

All Norwegian families with children under the age of 16 receive a yearly allowance for each child after the first. Financial aid is also available to help these families pay for housing. Large families with medium or low incomes pay little or no state taxes, and their local taxes are reduced. The government guarantees all workers an annual four-week vacation with full pay.

All Norwegians are required to participate in the national insurance program, which covers many welfare options. The plan includes retirement funds, job retraining, and financial aid. An insurance program provides free medical care and pays cash to employees when illness prevents them from working. Insured workers, their employers, and both national and local governments share the cost of all state insurance plans.

Health Care

Because it ensures a minimum standard of living for all its citizens, Norway has no severe health problems. Once plagued by polio and tuberculosis, Norwegians now face the risk of illnesses such as cancer and heart disease, which are common to wealthy countries. To combat tuberculosis and other contagious illnesses, all children receive complete vaccinations, and the entire population is given periodic tuberculin tests from infancy onward.

Measures of health have improved markedly in the twentieth century. In the 1890s, the average life expectancy for Norwegians was only 52 years, but by 1992 that figure had risen to 77 years. At the end of the nineteenth century, roughly 100 infants died out of every 1,000 born. In the mid-1990s an average of 6 babies died out of each 1,000 live births, which is among the best ratios in the world.

Photo by Hans-Olaf Pfannkuch

Norwegian families that have more than one child receive substantial financial assistance from the government—a practice that has improved the overall health of the population.

Because Norway's climate is too cool to grow many crops, the nation imports a healthy variety of fruits and vegetables to round out the Norwegian diet.

Photo by Kay Shaw Photography

Courtesy of Royal Norwegian Embassy

Three kindergarteners paint colorful artworks in their classroom. All Norwegians attend a minimum of nine years of school.

Like many industrialized nations, Norway is experiencing a very low birthrate in the late twentieth century. Fewer Norwegian women are choosing to have large families, if they have children at all. As a result, in 1995 authorities predicted that Norway's population would take 224 years to double.

With a national insurance plan that covers virtually all medical expenses, Norwegians pay very little directly toward health care. Although insurance is state-controlled, each community elects its own health board and public health officer. State and local officials jointly run hospitals. The country has a shortage of nursing and retirement homes, in part because a higher percentage of Norwegians are living beyond age 75 than ever before.

Education

With free education through the university level, nearly everyone in Norway can read and write. The first nine years of schooling—for children aged 7 to 16—are compulsory. Based on principles of equal opportunities for all, the Norwegian school system decides on one elementary curriculum and method of teaching for the whole country. Six years of primary school are followed by three years at the lower secondary level. Classes focus on math, science, nature study, Christianity, Norwegian and foreign languages, physical training, and social affairs.

Many students then continue with three years of upper secondary coursework. This includes two tracks: either gymnasium, which emphasizes general academic studies in preparation for university, or various kinds of vocational training. Although in theory all Norwegians are entitled to upper secondary education, a shortage of facilities—particularly in the area of vocational training—limits the number of admissions.

Norway has four universities—in Oslo, Bergen, Trondheim, and Tromsø—and several colleges, all of which are funded by the state. A network of regional colleges and technical and specialized institutions are part of the higher education system. In addition, laws require all cities and towns to have free public libraries, which the government partially supports.

Religion and Holidays

About 90 percent of the Norwegian people belong to the Church of Norway, which is Evangelical Lutheran. The state funds the institution, and the government appoints pastors and church officials. In 1956 the Storting passed a law allowing women to become pastors, and the state named the first female pastor in 1961.

Many Norwegians who consider themselves Lutherans do not participate in weekly services. A majority are baptized, confirmed, married, and buried in religious ceremonies, but fewer than 20 percent of Norwegian adults attend church more than five times a year. The constitution guarantees complete religious freedom. Most non-Lutheran churches in Norway are also Christian.

Stores and offices close in Norway on Christian holy days, such as Easter and Christmas. National independence is celebrated on Constitution Day—May 17. This date is set aside even though Norway did not gain complete self-rule until nearly a century after it enacted its first constitution on May 17, 1814. At Easter, many Norwegian families traditionally escape to cottages in the mountains for a week to enjoy the end of the skiing season.

Because summers in Norway are short, Norwegians celebrate Midsummer Eve,

After the first nine years of education, many Norwegians choose to attend a vocational school. Here, students learn how to create mouthwatering delicacies in their baking class.

Near Laerdalsøyri on the Sogne Fjord stands Borgund stave (wooden) church, which dates from about 1150. One of the oldest and best-preserved early Christian structures in Norway, the church exhibits a mix of Viking and Christian symbols, such as dragons and crosses.

Independent Picture Service

the brightest night of the year, which occurs in late June. People who own boats bring picnics out on the water to watch the night sun. At the first hint of dusk, Norwegians light bonfires along shorelines throughout the country.

Christmas is Norway's biggest annual festival. In addition to the religious significance of Christmas, the holiday falls during the shortest daylight hours of the year. Norwegians celebrated during this period long before Christianity arrived in the country. Ancient Norwegians believed that feasting soothed the powers of darkness and ensured a return of the sun.

In modern times, preparations for Christmas are made weeks in advance. At 5:00 P.M. on Christmas Eve, church bells toll, ringing in the holiday. After attending religious services, families join in a Christmas dinner and exchange gifts. The meal traditionally consists of roasted pork and sausage with sour cabbage or *lutefisk*— cod soaked in lye (a strong, salty liquor made from wood ashes). Christmas Day is typically a quiet time spent with family.

Photo by Liv Dahl

Many young children in Norway believe that the *Julenisse,* or Christmas elf, brings them presents from Santa Claus on Christmas Eve.

Courtesy of Gordon Haga

In the countryside, children dress up in masks and costumes during the week after Christmas and go door to door collecting treats. This boy has just returned from making the rounds.

Photo by Liv Dahl

Kransekake – a cone-shaped cake composed of almond-flavored cookie rings – is a traditional specialty served at Christmas, birthdays, and other Norwegian holidays.

Photo by Hans-Olaf Pfannkuch

A young boy eagerly devours a sweet treat. Coffee and snacks are customarily served to guests and at family gatherings in Norway.

On the evening of Midsummer Eve, Norwegians celebrate the longest day of the year by lighting bonfires. The number of hours of sunshine ranges from 24 in the north to 17.5 in the south.

On Boxing Day (the day after Christmas), a round of parties begins that lasts well into the new year.

Food

Living close to the sea, Norwegians historically have depended on fish and seafood for much of their diet. Cooks prepare fish in various ways, frequently serving it with boiled potatoes and vegetables at the main meal of the day—called *middag*—which most people eat between 4:00 and 6:00 P.M. Lingonberry jam—made from a tart, cranberrylike fruit—often accompanies *middag*.

Many of the fish dishes—such as fish balls and fish loaf—are very mild. Some of the national delicacies, however, are extremely salty and have a strong odor. *Gravet,* or smoked salmon, is a favorite, and some Norwegians savor *rakørret*—trout that has been aged for several months until it reaches a soft, buttery consistency with a slightly unpleasant smell. Mutton is the most common meat, and blood sausage (a spicy mixture of livestock's blood and flour) is a national specialty.

Norwegians eat *smørbrød,* or open-faced sandwiches, at three of their four daily meals.

45

Norwegians eat three other meals a day —breakfast, lunch, and supper. Each of these meals features *smørbrød*, or open-faced sandwiches. Smørbrød consist of bread or crackers layered with various combinations of cheese, jam, salmon spread, boiled egg, tomato, cucumber, sausage, herring, and sardines. Traditional desserts include fruit soup, *rømmegrøt* (cream pudding), and fresh berries during the summer. Coffee is perhaps the national drink in Norway, and guests usually are served coffee with cakes or smørbrød.

Language

Norwegian is part of the Germanic family of languages and draws from many European sources. Because mountains and fjords historically isolated Norwegian settlements from one another, numerous dialects exist in Norway.

Two forms of the Norwegian language— *bokmål* (book Norwegian) and *nynorsk* (new Norwegian)—are used officially and are very closely related. Bokmål developed during Norway's 400-year union with Denmark and is spoken in large towns, which were influenced strongly by Danish rule. Although spoken bokmål sounds very different from Danish, the written form is nearly identical to Danish. Created in reaction to Danish rule, nynorsk dates from the mid-1800s. This form combines elements from the major rural dialects to produce a more distinctly Norwegian language.

In the twentieth century, some Norwegian language experts have sought to streamline the two official tongues into one, called *samnorsk* (common Norwegian). The combined form would simplify communication between urban and rural areas and in the mass media, which now alternate between the two forms. Some Norwegians, however, feel strongly that bokmål and nynorsk—as well as the many dialects that influenced them—are part of the Norwegian heritage and should not be allowed to die out.

Literature

Norwegian literature can be divided into three historical periods. Old Norse (Norwegian-Icelandic) poems and legends originated in the Viking Age. Danish rule in Norway from about 1400 to 1814 heavily influenced writing now referred to as Norwegian-Danish literature. Liberation from Denmark in 1814 marks the beginning of the modern period, with nationalist works shaped by Norwegian concerns.

During the Old Norse period, Norwegian Vikings who settled in Iceland trans-

A statue in Gudbrandsdalen depicts Kristin Lavransdatter, the medieval heroine of three historical novels written in the twentieth century by Sigrid Undset. Set in Gudbrandsdalen during the fourteenth century, the trilogy traces Kristin's childhood, stormy marriage, and dedication to Christian service after the death of her husband.

mitted their beliefs, history, and myths through storytelling. In the thirteenth century, these tales began to appear in Icelandic manuscripts. The oldest known collection of poems is the *Poetic Edda*, which tells of the mythical gods and heroes of Scandinavia. Later Norse literature includes sagas, or prose epics, told by Icelanders. *Heimskringla*, a saga by Snorri Sturluson, chronicles the lives of Norwegian kings in the thirteenth century.

During the first two centuries of Danish rule, writing nearly ceased in Norway. Norwegian authors adopted Danish when it became the official language of Norway. By the eighteenth century, Norwegian writers were contributing significantly to Danish literature. Playwright Ludvig Holberg spent most of his life in Denmark and was the most distinguished author of the 1700s. His comedies are still performed on stages in Norway and Denmark.

Independent Picture Service

This representation of Ludvig Holberg, a Norwegian-born dramatist and historian, stands outside Oslo's National Theater. Flanking the statue of Holberg are two characters from his plays.

Independent Picture Service

At the request of Henrik Ibsen, Norwegian composer Edvard Grieg *(above)* wrote the music for the author's play *Peer Gynt*. Incorporating elements of Norwegian folk tunes, the work has delighted audiences around the world.

When Norway was transferred from Danish to Swedish control in 1814, a strong nationalist movement arose. Henrik Wergeland, who led the fight against Danish tradition, is considered the founder of Norwegian literature. Nationalism spurred an interest in writing down oral literature, which had existed among peasants for centuries. Peter Asbjørnsen and Jørgen Moe gathered and published these folktales.

In the second half of the nineteenth century, writers turned to realism and social criticism. Bjørnstjerne Bjørnson, Henrik Ibsen, Jonas Lie, and Alexander Kielland stood out among others in this new generation and became known as the Big Four. The dramatist Ibsen gained world fame for masterpieces such as *Peer Gynt, A Doll's House,* and *The Master Builder,* which probe human aspirations and limitations. The novels, plays, and poems of Bjørnson, who was also a political and social leader, earned him a Nobel Prize for literature in 1903.

An Icelandic manuscript from the fourteenth century depicts Saint Olav being struck down at the Battle of Stiklestad in 1030. The intricate patterns that frame the illustration are similar to those used in traditional wood carving.

Around the turn of the twentieth century, writers became concerned with the struggles of the individual, which were often expressed in lyric poetry. The novels of Knut Hamsun—such as *Hunger* and *Growth of the Soil*—explore social problems and portray people who reject modern society. Hamsun was awarded a Nobel Prize in 1920. In 1928 Sigrid Undset also won a Nobel Prize. She is best-known for her historical novels, especially the trilogy *Kristin Lavransdatter,* which is set in thirteenth-century Norway. Modern writers have continued to depict Norwegian life and history in realistic terms.

Nineteeth-century nationalist writers focused on Norwegian themes such as the rugged beauty of the land and the isolation of the individual from society.

The Arts

Among the oldest artistic works in Norway are Viking wood carvings. The Vikings decorated ships, buildings, wagons, sleighs, swords, and other objects with intricate carvings of animals—especially dragons, horses, snakes, and swans. Floral and geometric patterns were also popular designs. Most of the Viking artifacts have been found at burial sites.

With the arrival of Christianity, Norwegians developed their own form of religious architecture in stave (wooden) churches. These structures retain some of the Viking artistic themes, but they also display Christian influences from other parts of Europe. Constructed on stone foundations to prevent moisture in the ground from rotting the wood, about 30 stave churches still stand in Norway. Christian and Viking influences also mingled in other art forms throughout the next several centuries.

When the nationalist movement arose in literature in the nineteenth century, visual arts underwent a similar change. Paintings of Norwegian landscapes and depictions of daily life became popular. Johan Christian Dahl led the development of a Norwegian style in painting. He also introduced the mountain as a symbol that would recur in the works of later Norwegian artists and writers. Adolf Tidemand and Hans Gude followed in the nationalist footsteps of Dahl.

In the late 1800s, Frits Thaulow, Christian Krohg, and Erik Werenskiold painted realistic images of Norway and its people. Edvard Munch, one of Norway's greatest painters, also began working during this period, but he soon rejected the detailed realism of his contemporaries. Instead, Munch pioneered the Norwegian expressionist movement, which uses objects and events to arouse inner emotions. His most famous works—including *The Scream, The Sick Child, The Vampire,* and *In Hell, Self-portrait*—depict individuals who are tormented and isolated.

The Monolith, a sculpture by Gustav Vigeland in Oslo's Frogner Park, contains 121 figures struggling toward the summit. Carved from a single block of stone, the column is 60 feet tall and weighs 200 tons.

Gustav Vigeland, a sculptor and contemporary of Munch, also used expressionism. Frogner Park in Oslo contains about

The later paintings of Edvard Munch (1863-1944), such as *Ladies on the Quay,* reveal a much more positive attitude toward life than his earlier works, which focus on sickness and death.

150 of his massive symbolic figures representing various aspects and stages of life. Twentieth-century Norwegian art has become increasingly abstract.

Cross-country skiing is a favorite winter pastime in Norway.

Sports and Recreation

Outdoor activities are an important part of Norwegian life. Many Norwegians are nature enthusiasts and have easy access to recreational areas. Hiking in the mountains or on wooded hillsides is a favorite activity. In the winter, Norwegians ski across snow-covered wilderness. On some trails, people can ski or walk for days, spending nights at cabins located at regular intervals along the way.

Skiing is the country's national sport, and it may have originated in Norway thousands of years ago as a means of transport. Three kinds of skiing—downhill, cross-country, and slalom (which creates a zigzag pattern in the snow)—are popular. Ice-skating is also a favorite winter sport, and some people play bandy, a form of hockey. Competitive skiing and speed skating appear on television.

Soccer is the nation's main summer sport, and it attracts thousands of spectators each season. Other fair-weather activities include boating, fishing, rowing, swimming, and cycling.

The development of Norway's economy has depended in part on building a transportation network. The country's rugged terrain poses a serious challenge to road and railway planners, and the nation uses boats to move both goods and people along the coast.

4) The Economy

Norway's economy has undergone rapid industrial growth since World War II. Two factors—the development of hydroelectric power since 1900 and the discovery of oil in the 1960s—have aided economic expansion. Although economic activity slowed in the 1980s, Norwegians continued to enjoy one of the highest standards of living in the world. If the gross national product (GNP)—the value of goods and services produced in a year—were divided equally among all the nation's citizens, each person would receive more than $26,000.

Private enterprise dominates the economy, but state regulations affect ownership. For example, the government limits the disposal of industrial waste and supervises the activities of banks and insurance companies. The Working Environment

Act of 1977 requires employers to provide job security and to limit working hours to a maximum of 9 hours per day. The law also forbids laborers to work more than 200 hours of overtime per year.

The export of oil from the North Sea greatly benefited Norway's economy. After the price of oil fell in 1986, however, rising unemployment spurred the Norwegian government to develop new mainland industries. While this move may reduce Norway's dependence on income from oil exports, few measures have yet been taken to reshape Norway's economy.

Manufacturing

Because Norway lacks large reserves of coal to fuel factories, it developed

Courtesy of Royal Norwegian Embassy

With vast expanses of forest, Norway has a thriving paper industry.

industries later than many other European countries. Once the nation began to harness hydropower from its rivers, however, it had a cheap source of electricity. This energy base spurred rapid industrialization in the twentieth century. Early industries in Norway depended on local raw materials, such as iron ore, timber, and fish. Since the discovery of oil in 1969, a petrochemical industry has also arisen.

About half the nation's factories are located near Oslo, and manufacturing contributes roughly 15 percent to Norway's gross domestic product—that is, the money earned within the country each year. In the early 1970s, this figure neared 30 percent. Wage increases and economic conditions, however, made Norwegian products more expensive and therefore less competitive on the international market. The discovery and production of oil has helped to offset the decline in manufacturing.

Hydroelectricity remains the principal source of power in Norway. The major in-

Independent Picture Service

This dam in the Telemark region powers a hydroelectric plant. Most of Norway's industries rely on hydroelectricity to power their operations.

Many metal and chemical industries in Norway exist only because of the availability of a cheap source of power—hydroelectricity. For example, this plant near the coast imports bauxite (a raw material that Norway lacks), processes it into aluminum, and then exports it immediately.

dustrial users of hydropower fall into three main groups—electrometallurgical, electrochemical, and timber processing. Metallurgy (the science and technology of metals) is dominated by smelting works. These factories melt raw materials—such as aluminum oxide, nickel, copper, chromium, and manganese—to extract the metal and to create alloys (mixtures of metals). Norway imports most of the raw materials it refines and then exports them immediately. After Canada, Norway is the largest exporter of metal in the world.

Norway is also a large-scale producer and exporter of chemical products. For example, Norsk Hydro, Norway's biggest industrial concern, is among the world's largest producers of fertilizer. Petrochem-

ical plants refine some of the nation's crude oil and natural gas for export or for use in the manufacture of other products. Although the ship-building industry declined in the 1980s, some ship-building companies shifted their production to oil rigs and other equipment for the North Sea oil fields. Other Norwegian manufacturers produce machinery, pulp and paper, and textiles.

Oil and Energy

In 1969 Phillips Petroleum, a U.S. company, discovered the Ekofisk oil fields in the Norwegian section of the North Sea. By 1975 Norway was exporting oil products, which greatly boosted the

53

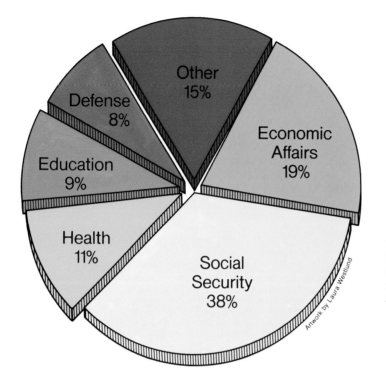

This chart shows the percentage of Norway's budget spent on various social and economic concerns. (Data taken from *World Economic Data, 3rd edition.*)

For more than 300 years, Røros thrived on copper mining. The town now derives most of its income from agriculture and tourism. A rich history and colorful architecture attract numerous visitors each year.

Courtesy of Royal Norwegian Embassy

The shipbuilding plant in Haugesund manufactures oil-drilling rigs as well as boats. The discovery of vast quantities of oil in the 1970s led the nation to restructure its industries to accommodate the new resource. Within a decade, oil had become Norway's most important money-earner.

economy. In 1986 revenues from oil amounted to nearly 20 percent of the gross domestic product, despite a drop in the price of oil. This new source of revenue permitted Norway to further expand an already strong social welfare system.

The nation's oil resources are located offshore on the continental shelf. As of the early 1990s, most of the drilling was taking place in the North Sea off Norway's southwestern coast, but considerable reserves are known to exist beyond the Arctic Circle. The government has announced plans to extend exploration into the Barents Sea. The major oil and gas fields – Frigg, Ekofisk, and Statfjord – together account for 90 percent of Norway's total crude oil production.

The Norwegian government controls much of the oil industry. After the discovery of petroleum, the legislature voted to limit annual production to conserve the oil fields. In 1972 the government created a company named Statoil to oversee all aspects of the industry, from exploration and drilling to transport, processing, and selling of petroleum and natural gas. Factories refine only about one-fifth of the nation's crude oil, but Statoil has plans to expand the refinery at Mongstad, and the company is building a huge industrial complex at Karstø.

Most of Norway's gas and oil output is exported. The country provides about 14 percent of western Europe's gas requirements—a figure that is expected to rise. For nearly all of its own energy needs, the nation relies on hydroelectricity. With numerous mountain streams and rivers, Norway produces more hydroelectric power in relation to its population than any other country in the world.

Foreign Trade

A shortage of natural resources forced early Norwegians to exchange fish and timber for other goods from foreign lands. As a result, Norway has a long history as a trading nation. In modern times, the country depends on international trade for much of its prosperity. Norway's merchant fleet is among the world's largest shipping lines.

Norway's export trade changed dramatically in the 1970s with the development of petroleum and natural gas reserves in the North Sea. These two products account for nearly half of all goods sold abroad. Other major exports include machinery, ships, aluminum, chemicals, pulp and paper products, and food items. Imports include machinery, transportation equipment, petroleum products, chem-

At the Rafnes refinery, workers process crude oil into materials that will be used in chemical industries. Norway exports both crude and refined petroleum.

Independent Picture Service

One of the biggest ports in Norway, Bergen is a center for the nation's trading activities.

icals, foodstuffs, and ores. Norway trades most heavily with Great Britain, Sweden, and Germany. The United States, Denmark, and Finland are also important trading partners.

Agriculture and Forestry

Until the twentieth century, agriculture was a mainstay of the Norwegian economy and the most important source of employment. By the mid-1990s, however, agriculture accounted for only about 3 percent of the GDP and employed about 6 percent of the work force.

Although most Norwegians now work in the manufacturing, oil, or service sectors of

Courtesy of Minneapolis Public Library and Information Center

Farmers hang hay, one of Norway's main crops, over poles to dry before it is used for livestock feed.

57

the economy, agricultural output has increased in the last century. The growth is due to mechanized equipment, fertilizers, improved animal feed and breeding techniques, and education. Furthermore, government funding and cooperative organizations—in which groups of farmers can buy equipment and sell goods collectively—have eased the financial burdens that once plagued agricultural workers.

The government oversees the welfare of farming to ensure its continuation. The nation's rugged terrain leaves only 3 percent of the land suitable for cultivation. Nevertheless, Norwegians place a priority on being as self-sufficient in food as possible. Consequently, agriculture manages to provide about half of the nation's foodstuffs, and Norway buys the rest from other countries. Although government assistance is extensive, most farmers own their land and work relatively small plots that average about 20 acres.

With so much mountainous terrain, Norway can cultivate only about one-third of the area that is suitable for farming. The rest is used as pasture for livestock. Livestock raising and dairy farming are concentrated in Vestlandet and Nord Norge. The broad valleys of Østlandet and Trøndelag are best suited for crops. Much of the cultivated farmland provides livestock feed, which includes most of Norway's barley, hay, and oats. The nation imports grain for human consumption. Other food crops include potatoes, fruits, and vegetables. The supply of meat and dairy products meets domestic demand, but Norway must import fruits and vegetables in addition to grain.

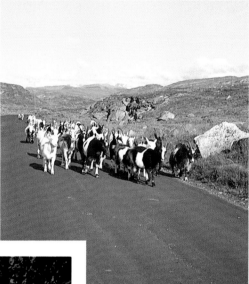

Photo by Hans-Olaf Pfannkuch

Photo by Kay Shaw Photography

Goats *(above)* graze on Norway's barren highland plateaus. After milking the animals, farmers sell the liquid to factories that manufacture cheese. Most crop-growing farms are located in Norway's fertile mountain valleys.

Courtesy of Harlan V. Anderson

For centuries, Norwegian farmers have cut timber during the winter to boost their incomes when they are not working in the fields.

Photo by Liv Dahl

Norwegian farmers—especially in the west and the north—have also traditionally relied on fishing to supplement their incomes. Here, customers purchase shrimp at dockside.

59

Fish processing employs many workers in coastal areas.

The Norwegian government has sought to mechanize the fishing industry, which would eliminate the part-time role of the fisher-farmer. Farmers in the west and north have strongly opposed these efforts. They continue to bring in small catches using traditional wooden boats.

To supplement their incomes, some Norwegian farmers also engage in commercial forestry. Land owned by farmers contains half the nation's productive forests, which are located primarily in the counties of Nord-Trøndelag, Hedmark, Oppland, and Buskerud.

Most of the timber is softwood—including birch, pine, and spruce—and is used in wood processing. Pulp and paper products account for about 8 percent of the earnings from exports. Logging could not be increased without using up the forests, which government regulations protect. As a result, the nation imports timber from Sweden and Finland to keep its processing plants operating at full capacity.

Fishing

Norway has a long history as a fishing nation. Although this activity now earns less than 1 percent of the yearly GNP, Norway ranks as one of the world's leading fishing countries, providing 3.4 percent of the total global catch.

The number of fishermen registered in Norway has dropped by more than half since the 1960s. Nevertheless, the size of the catch has increased because more fishermen now work year-round at only one occupation. Furthermore, bigger vessels and more effective equipment enable crews to take in larger hauls in less time. The fleet has extended its area of operation to the shores of Newfoundland, an island off the eastern coast of Canada.

Norwegian crews take in about 2.5 million tons of fish per year. The catch includes, in order of cash value, cod, capelin, coalfish, and shrimp. Much of the volume is processed for export. Fish farming of salmon and trout in the fjords and inlets along the coast has also become an important industry. In the 1980s, the export value of salmon and trout surpassed that of cod. Most of Norway's hatcheries are located in the counties of Hordaland, Møre og Romsdal, and Sør-Trøndelag.

Some types of marine life once caught by Norwegian fishermen are in danger of extinction. To promote the continued existence of these species, the government either forbids or strictly regulates the catches. For example, quotas now restrict the size of hauls of herring, and fishermen have largely replaced herring with capelin. Once a renowned whaling nation, Norway temporarily ceased commercial whaling to allow these mammals to replenish their numbers. Commercial whaling was resumed in 1993, however, against bans set by the International Whaling Commission.

Transportation

Although Norway's rugged terrain makes building roads and railroads difficult and expensive, the nation has developed a broad and efficient system of transportation. A network of roads, railways, and water routes serves the country.

Most Norwegian households have a car, but public transit is well developed. Express buses link the biggest towns, with the longest routes running between Oslo and Hammerfest and between Fauske and Kirkenes. Of more than 56,000 miles of roads, about two-thirds are paved. Because the terrain is gentler in the east than in the west, the road network is the best developed in Østlandet. Many roads curve along fjords and mountains and pass through tunnels and over bridges.

For centuries, water transit was the most effective means of transportation in Norway. In modern times, ferryboats provide a vital link between motor routes that stop at the edge of the fjords. Vessels also travel the coastline. The Coastal Express is a boat system that has transported passengers and cargo to points between Bergen and Kirkenes since the late 1800s. Express vessels are equipped to carry cars so that passengers can take the boat one way and drive back. Some of the passenger boats are hydrofoils, which can travel much faster than other vessels.

Independent Picture Service

Numerous bridges in Norway span rivers and fjords and link island communities to the mainland. At the northern town of Tromsø, an aerial cableway carries people to the top of 1,380-foot Mount Storsteinen.

Independent Picture Service

Noted for their quickness, hydrofoils have metal plates, or fins, that lift the boats out of the water as they gain speed.

61

Road building in Norway poses many difficulties for construction engineers, who have carved some routes out of sheer rock.

The opening of the first rail line in 1854 signaled the beginning of increased mobility within Norway. Today, more than half the nation's 2,600 miles of track run on electric power. Operated by the Norwegian State Railway, express and local trains branch out from Oslo in all directions and connect the country to Sweden and Denmark. Trondheim and Narvik are linked to Swedish railways, and the Nordland Line transports passengers from Trondheim to Fauske and Bodø in Nord Norge. Commuter trains service Oslo, Bergen, and Trondheim.

With over 40 airports, Norway relies increasingly on airways to cover the vast, mountainous distances within the country. Scandinavian Airlines (SAS), which is owned jointly by Norway, Sweden, and Denmark, offers international service. Helicopters provide connections between North Sea oil installations and the mainland.

The Future

Norway's continued prosperity depends in part on international factors beyond its control. World trade issues and the price of oil greatly affect the Norwegian economy. By continuing to expand industries, Norway can help to offset concerns about petroleum and commerce.

The Flåm Line winds its way through the narrow Flåm Valley, climbing nearly 3,000 feet in just two miles. The roller-coaster effect of this railway has made it popular among tourists.

Well-designed social programs have ensured a comfortable lifestyle with equal opportunities for all Norwegian citizens. The discovery of oil allowed Norway to further expand its welfare system. Uncertain prospects for future oil revenues, however, could endanger some of the services upon which Norwegian society is built and could create a higher unemployment rate. As a result, the nation has begun to explore ways to adjust its economic and social welfare policies without sacrificing its high standard of living. The challenge of balancing services and trade will occupy Norwegians in the coming decades.

Photo by Josh Kohnstamm

Photo by A. Waldo

Steep mountains and the waters of the Sogne Fjord flank the town of Flåm. The historical isolation of Norwegian communities and the nation's low population density have helped to shape a strong sense of independence. This national character trait will influence Norwegian leaders as they face the challenges of the twenty-first century.

Index